Birkenhead

Park

by

Jean McInniss

First published 1984 by Countyvise Limited, 14 Appin Road, Birkenhead, Wirral, Merseyside CH41 9HH.

ISBN 0 907768 75 X

Copyright © Jean McInnis, 1984

Photoset and printed by Birkenhead Press Limited, 14 Appin Road, Birkenhead, Wirral, Merseyside CH41 9HH.

Dedicated to the memory
of my great aunts,
Harriet and Susie Thomas,
formerly of Claughton.

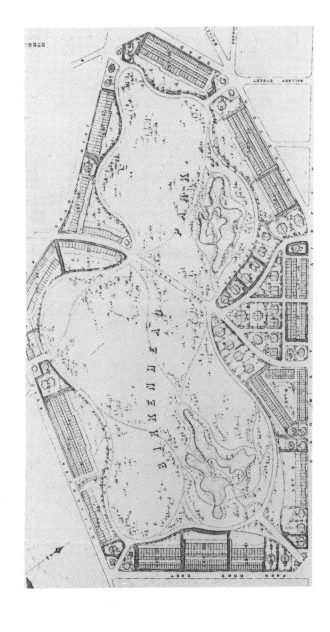

CONTENTS

		page
Section 1	A Challenge	7
Section 2	The Land and the Town	9
Section 3	Park Design	11
Section 4	Getting Down to Work	13
Section 5	Entrances and Lodges	15
Section 6	Perimeter Housing	20
Section 7	The Park is Opened	22
Section 8	Leisure-time Pursuits	26
Section 9	Echoing England's History	36
Section 10	Reflections Today	37
Quote from	'The Stanger's Guide' — 1847	41
Quote from	'Walks and Talks of an American Farmer in England' 1850	41
Quote from	'Memories of Birkenhead' 1892	43
Quote from	Board of Health 'Minutes of Information'. 1852	43
Sir Joseph Paxton - biographical details.................		44
Sir William Jackson - biographical details...............		45
Appendix A	Bands performing in the Park between 1894/1916...........................	46
Appendix B	Football teams playing in the Park between 1894/1922...........................	47
Appendix C	Cricket teams playing in the Park between 1893/1932...........................	48
Appendix D	Wages and prices current in the years between 1893/1919...........................	49
Appendix E	Rules when Fishing in the Park Lakes. 1889 .	52
Appendix F	Order of Architectural merit — buildings on Park perimeter	53
Appendix G	Extracts from notes made by Mr. Edward Hubbard re architecture, etc	54
Appendix H	Some of the people living in the new park property, circa 1860	57
Bibliography		58
Acknowledgements		59
Friends of Birkenhead Park		61

1. A CHALLENGE

It was Sir William Jackson who first thought of it.[1] Birkenhead should have its own park. In these days we take parks for granted. Birkenhead is particularly well-endowed with them, but then, in the 1840s, it was quite a revolutionary idea. Parks were for the landed gentry, or were grants of royal land for the use of commoners. But a park from the people to the people — this was entirely new.[2] As for the site that Sir William Jackson had in mind, not far from Claughton Manor where he had lately come to live, a lesser man than Joseph Paxton would have laughed at the impossibility of it when first approached. Joseph Paxton, when he and Sir William inspected that low-lying swamp with its unhealthy mists, was head gardener at Chatsworth House in Derbyshire. He had been born in 1803 near to another great house at Woburn. Later he was to decline the opportunity of being Queen Victoria's head gardener at Windsor. But it wasn't just as a famous gardener that Joseph Paxton was to make his name, he was a great engineer and architect as well. He was to design the Crystal Palace. After that he was knighted. This stupendous glass hall, four times the area of St. Peter's in Rome, was used for the Great Exhibition of 1851 when Britain showed off her products to an admiring world. You can see that Sir William Jackson had approached a very gifted man with his idea of a park for Birkenhead.[3]

There seemed no way that that low-lying marsh could be turned into a park.[4] Fortunately Sir William Jackson was not a man to be easily put off. Before he left, Paxton had been persuaded to sketch out a rough plan of how his host's ambitious scheme might be brought about. The proposed fee for the job was £800.[5] Maybe in the end it was the tremendous challenge to his skill and ingenuity that Paxton couldn't resist.[6]

---

1. Sir William Jackson, Bart, a Liverpool business man, was one of the Town Commissioners. See Biographical Note page 45

2. The Derby Arboretum, (1840), was the first park to be specifically designed for and owned by the public, but it was the result of a private benefaction on the part of a wealthy manufacturer, Joseph Strutt, who instructed J.C. Loudon to prepare a design for a piece of ground which belonged to him and which he wanted to present to the Corporation of Derby.

Princes Park, Liverpool, a public park and private suburb, immediately preceded Birkenhead Park. It was an undertaking of speculative development and public philanthropy on the part of Richard Vaughan Yates, a member of a wealthy Liverpool family. Laid out by Joseph Paxton in 1842, it was his first essay in park design. (Regent's Park and St. James' Park were the progenitors of Princes Park and of all other later suburban park layouts.)

3. Sir Joseph Paxton is chiefly remembered as the designer of the Crystal Palace, but he was one of the greatest gardeners of the 19th century as well as being a skilful engineer, an architect, a journalist and author, and a business man. See Biographical Note page 44

4. See extract from the Minutes of Information, published by the Board of Health in January 1852. page 43

5. William Jackson, at a meeting of the Improvement Commissioners on August 1st, 1843, said he had engaged Paxton for £800 and a Superintendent was being employed under him.

6. Paxton wrote to his wife — "I walked at least 30 miles to make myself master of the locality etc. This is not a very good situation for a park as the land is generally poor but of course it will redound more to my credit and honour to make something handsome and good out of these materials, indeed I am not altogether sorry that it is as it is, for it will suit my ingenuity to work to overcome the difficulty."
Quoted by George F. Chadwick in "The Works of Joseph Paxton", page 51.

2. THE LAND AND THE TOWN

We know a little of the history of the land on which it was proposed to lay the park. It must have been used by our very distant ancestors. Up to the end of the last century there were two mounds near to Ashville Road. They were on an open space between the plantations. Children had great fun playing on them.[1] They became bare and unsightly. One day the Coroporation carts arrived. The workmen got busy. The hills were gradually taken away. Now it is thought that these 'bonks' as they were nick-named, were covering underground burial chambers. They could have contained bronze age implements and pottery. A small bronze-age axe head was discovered near the park band-stand.

Much later in time the monks from Birkenhead Priory held the land. When the smaller monasteries were dissolved in 1536, a man called Ralph Worsley was to become Lord of the Manor of Claughton.

In the 17th century the land was known as 'the Lowerfields'. A yeoman farmer called Wilson left it to his son Richard in his Will. It was described as low-lying and often waterlogged.

At the time that Sir William Jackson had his idea of having a park, a man called Francis Richard Price owned most of the township of Claughton. The land that Sir William and Joseph Paxton inspected was common land. It was criss-crossed by rough lanes. There was good gorse cover for foxes. Although it was poor quality and unproductive there was a small farm in the area. This farm belonged to a Mrs. Hannah Mutch who also kept a beerhouse at the junction of two lanes. Badger-baiting, rat-killing and dog-fights were held on her premises.

When the first ever census was held in 1801 only 110 people lived in Birkenhead. It was just a scatter of farms and cottages with a sea-side area near the ruins of the former Benedictine Priory. But twenty years later the steam-ferries began a regular service. Birkenhead was now to become a dormitory town. Well-to-do commuters settled in Birkenhead, which was a green and pleasant area. They crossed the river to work in Liverpool. In 1824 William Laird purchased land. He established a shipyard. Gone was the sea-side now. By 1831 you have to multiply the original 110 people no less than 26 times. Only ten years later, in 1841, the population had again trebled.[2] Birkenhead has gone on growing ever since.

In 1824/5, William Laird had instructed J. Gillespie Graham of Edinburgh to plan a new town. A plain grid was designed.[3] It was 1 mile by $\frac{1}{4}$ mile. The streets were laid out in long, straight, wide roads.

In 1833, when William IV was on the throne, Town Commissioners were appointed to govern Birkenhead, including Claughton.[4] The streets were now continued westwards. They reached the common land where Sir William Jackson wanted the park to be. The boundaries of the park were fixed by the projection of this grid-iron layout. Beyond the site, the ground began to rise pleasantly towards Claughton ridge. This hinterland favoured eventual surburban development. Around where Park Road West is today it was open countryside. Some people thought it stupid to plan a park next to the country. You had to be far-sighted to realise that the town was going to keep on growing. Sir William Jackson must have known that when the last of the countryside had gone, Birkonians were going to need this park.

---

1. See page 43

2. The town of Birkenhead exists because of the 19th century with its industrial expansion. Like Barrow-in-Furness and Fleetwood, it is in an esturial position and was deliberately planned from the beginning.

3. A plain grid plan was often used when designing new settlements.

4. Sixty Town Commissioners were appointed. About half of these were Liverpool businessmen. Their task was to govern Birkenhead, including Claughton, and to arrange for the paving, lighting, watching, cleansing and otherwise improvement of the township. They also had to regulate the police and establish a market.

3. PARK DESIGN

Before the Industrial Revolution many people lived in the country. They earned their living in their homes, or in the surrounding fields. As the 18th century gathered momentum and the 19th century dawned, choice or force of circumstances led folk to seek work in the mills and factories of local towns. This exodus from the countryside continued over many decades. It coincided with a tremendous growth in the population. Up until this time there had not been any great need for public parks.   There were parks attached to the stately homes of the wealthy. There were the royal parks to which public access was in some cases available.   Once people were herded together in towns, often living in poor and unsanitary conditions, an urgent need for 'breathing spaces' arose.

The parks of the post-renaissance had been rather artificial-looking places. Extensively wooded, they often held aviaries or contained caged wild beasts. Garden design had been formal and geometrical. Occasionally there had been raised terraces and gazebos.

When Birkenhead Park was planned a spirit of romanticism held sway. This affected books and music, paintings and architecture as well as the laying out of new parks. The longing to recapture the supposed peace and tranquility of country scenes was expressed in many poems and paintings of this period. It was just one aspect of romanticism which also dismissed the more classical and formalized structures in favour of a new freedom.

The first early stirrings of romanticism manifested in landscape design. It was something which England gave to the world. As early as 1730 formal gardens were going. Lancelot Brown, (1716-1783), known as 'Capability' Brown, who laid out the gardens at Kew, had revived a 'natural' style of landscape gardening. The degree of regularity to be found in earlier landscape gardens, gave way to the more irregular, 'serpentine', line of beauty. Paxton, when designing Birkenhead Park, continued fully in the mid-18th century spirit. He was trying to recreate a pastoral scene. He wanted it to look like countryside at its best. Contrived and artificial formality would not have been in keeping with the spirit of the age. After the Second World War, an area of the Upper Park was restored. It had been used for allotments to help the war effort. The rose gardens and trellises and formal pathways raised an outcry from the traditionalists. They wanted to see the more naturalistic layout envisaged by Paxton restored.

Birkenhead Park, with its informal, gently picturesque, surburban landscape, is post-Reptonian. That is, it is in a style pioneered by

Repton — (and John Nash, designer of the Regent's Park villages, circa 1825.) Humphry Repton, (1752-1811), a professional landscape gardener, was to have a considerable influence on 19th century styles. He allied the Brownian landscape park with the 'picturesque'. Repton would also look to find the 'genius of the place', and had an eye to the practical as well as to the overall 'picture' that he was creating, and utility had a part to play in the overall design. His 'mantle' fell upon John Claudius Loudon, (1783-1843), with his interests in horticulture, botany and architecture. Loudon allied garden 'art' and botany. Coupling science with art led to a style called the 'gardenesque'. Loudon's writings on the subject derived in a large measure from Repton's later works. Repton preceded Loudon by some thirty years. Paxton succeeded Loudon by some twenty years. The technically ingenius Paxton was quite happy to work in styles already pioneered and found to be acceptable. He put Loudon's ideas into practice, modifying and adapting them as the need arose. He also worked within the Reptonian basis of achieving a balanced relationship between pleasure-ground and park. In turn, Paxton's influence was carried on via the work of the men whom he had trained. His Superintendent at Birkenhead, Edward Kemp, was one. It was not until 1870, five years after Paxton's death that further original theories were to be introduced by a man called William Robinson.

The Palm House, Upper Park. Later the Conservatory occupied the site.

12

4. GETTING DOWN TO WORK

Birkenhead Park was to be the first park in this country to be provided at public expense. The Act of Parliament giving the Royal Assent was passed in April 1843. 226 acres were purchased. 125 acres were for public use. The remainder was to be sold as house plots.

The area of parkland was cut in two by a transverse road which was called Ashville Road. The Claughton Village half of the park was to be known as the Upper Park. The other portion of the park was to be known as the Lower Park.

The first sod was cut in 1844. From then onwards, for around three years, 1,000 men worked hard to make that unattractive area into a sylvan countryside. First the marshes were drained. Eight acres of lakes were formed. The spoil from the excavations was deposited around the lakes in hillocks of various heights forming valleys in between. Later the hillocks were planted out. The mounds in the Lower Park were made higher than those in the Upper Park. They were about 20 to 30 feet and they now have tall trees. The lakes were made with little bays and promontories. They advance and recede sinuously. So do the paths around their edges which at one moment are near to the water and then move away from it. The lakes in both parks have a central island. In the Upper Park the visual effect can give the illusion that the waterway is a meandering river. The design of the lakes and their perimeter is supposed to be Paxton at his best. There is a variation of 60 feet between the Claughton side of the park and the main entrance. The land slopes away from Claughton fairly evenly. The lakes were put in the more natural lower position. One has now disappeared. It was a small, figure-of-eight lake in the Lower Park. It was adjacent to the driveway and near to the path which leads into Park Road South. It is now a sunken garden. This small lake was used for curling and ice skating in the cold winters around the turn of the century. For this purpose the water level was kept low. Stand and look down on this garden. In your mind's eye can you see those skaters of so long ago enjoying themselves? Perhaps the neighbouring trees and houses remember their laughter and merriment!

Mr. Edward Kemp was a very important gentleman in those early days of the park. It was he who implemented Joseph Paxton's plan. He supervised the laying out of the park — and later other parks in the area. For over forty years afterwards he remained on as the head park-keeper.[1]

The total cost of laying out the park and the gardens, including levelling the ground, excavating the lakes and the planting, was in the region of £70,000. This included a stone boathouse, a temple-like bandstand and a Swiss bridge. There were three bridges altogether in the Lower Park. One was called the Rustic bridge. The third bridge was made of cast-iron. It was a symbolic bridge of that era. It represented one aspect of the Industrial Revolution and it was the Industrial Revolution which had created the need for public parks.[2]

---

1. Kemp had been employed and trained by Paxton at Chatsworth House. He came to Birkenhead in 1843 when he was 25 years old. He was the first tenant of the Italian Lodge in Park Road South. Later he lived at 74 Park Road West where his monogram 'E.S.K.' may still be seen on the front chimney stack and the date 1859. (The 'S' was the initial of his wife, Sophia.) Kemp inherited the current scientific fascination for botany. There are still unusual shrubs and special varieties of holly in the garden and an ancient Spanish weeping oak, similar to one in Kew Gardens. An expert in his own right, Kemp went into practice on his own account in 1847 and amongst many local parks and gardens, laid out Hesketh Park in Southport. One of the men who carried on the influence of Paxton's work, he shared in the development of the 'Gardenesque' theory. His book, "How to Lay out a Garden" ran to three editions. The last, published in 1864, was a comprehensive illustrated volume in which he drew on his experience in laying out over forty private gardens since commencing practice. He died on Monday, 2nd March, 1891 at the age of 73 years and was buried at Flaybrick.

2. The lake in the Upper Park was also planned with two bridges affording a pedestrian route across the island.

5. ENTRANCES AND LODGES

A gently undulating, serpentine driveway, three miles long, snaking around the perimeter of the park, divided it off from the building land. This carriageway was for pleasure traffic only. The park was bounded by town roads from which service to the villas could be gained and there was Ashville Road, bisecting the park, which connected town and dock areas with the salubrious reaches of prospective residential development. Within the park greater and lesser footpaths linked all parts to the town roads. One elevated pathway in the Lower Park commands a panoramic view of the lake.

In Ashville Road, four entrances were made into the park. Five other gates also gave access to the carriage drive. The gates, bearing the arms of Birkenhead Priory, the railings and their housings, to a uniform design throughout, and some of the park lodges, were constructed under Paxton's supervision, by a young Liverpool architect, Lewis Hornblower.[1]

There was a hierarchy of stone piers throughout the park which was based on the relative importance of the various entrances. The largest, chunkiest piers were on the major gateways. Lesser ones were for the pedestrian entrances, with a smaller design for house entrances.[2]

There is a possibility that as Hornblower was very young when commissioned, he may have been supervised, when designing the lodges, by John Robertson, the architect who had drawn Paxton's plan for the park. (Paxton had not received architectural training and Robertson had been his architectural assistant at Chatsworth). For some years following March 1829, Robertson had worked for John Claudius Loudon as an architectural draughtsman. By 1840 he was designing villas for Edensor, Paxton's model village at Chatsworth. Loudon published books and magazines. His "Encyclopaedia of Cottage; Farm and Villa Architecture" contained drawings by Robertson of houses similar to our park lodges, being in the Edensor styles, that is Italianate, Norman, Elizabethan and Swiss styles of architecture. "Loudon's publications . . . helped to mould the visual tastes of early Victorian England."[3]

Nine lodges were proposed in all. The two lodges that form part of the main entrance into the park, and four others, were completed before 1847. Two others were built shortly afterwards. Central Lodge is in Ashville Road. The Gothic Lodge in Park Road West is castellated. Park Road East Lodge is neo-Elizabethan. The Italian Lodge in Park Road South has a belvedere tower. The Norman Lodges, neighbouring Norman Street, are a Greek Revival pair. The Gothic Lodge is not shown on a map dated 1858 and maybe later than the others.

The main entrance into the park, designed by Gillespie Graham, was put at the junction where Park Road North meets Park Road East. In the last century, Birkenhead being very much smaller, this spot with its approach from Conway Street, was nearest to the then town. Set back on the splay, it must have seemed a very impressive structure. There is Loudonish precedent here as well. It is not unlike a grand triumphal Roman Arch, and although Italianate, proclaims supreme Victorian self-confidence. The frontage measures 125 feet with a central carriageway through an arch of 18 feet span being 43 feet in height. Smaller pedestrian archways are flanked by two-storey lodges. Columns are placed in couples between each arch. The top centre carries the arms of Birkenhead. The original wrought-iron gates were ornamented with the armorial bearings of Birkenhead Priory. This entrance put Birkenhead into the same league as some famous capital cities with similar structures. It can be said to vie with the Marble Arch in London and the Arc de Triomphe in Paris!

The lodges and other park buildings, like the bridges crossing the lakes, were all part of Paxton's scheme.

---

1. Probably the best preserved stretch of the original railings fronts Park High School in Park Road South.

Some of the spear-heads of a section of the railings in Ashville Road were removed when painting was taking place.

The pedestrian gate into the Upper Park from Ashville Road survives. The arms of Birkenhead Priory can still be seen on the lock portion. One or two of the original gates still exist on the villas.

Much iron-work fell victim to the 2nd World War munitions factories.

2. The replaced gateposts are not identical to the original. Certain details have not been exactly followed.

3. From Edward Hubbard's notes for the Victorian Society. 1973.

Mr. N.G. Holden has, over many years, collected many postcards of the park. We are grateful to him for allowing us to reproduce a number of these in this book. A selection follows and more will be found on pages 38, 39 and 40.

FROM GLYN HOLDEN'S POSTCARD COLLECTION

18

Swiss Bridge, Birkenhead

FROM GLYN HOLDEN'S POSTCARD COLLECTION

A view in Birkenhead Park.

6. PERIMETER HOUSING

Joseph Paxton had a good head for business as well as having all his other talents. Sir William Jackson was a business man too. They realised that houses built around the park perimeter would be sought after and be a good investment. There were precedents. Regent's Park, laid out in 1814 by John Nash (1752-1835), had crescents and villas and terraces, and Liverpool's Princes Park suburban housing.

Francis Richard Price sold the poor land for 1/- a yard. The total price was £69,690. £60,000 was borrowed from Parliament by the Town Commissioners. But as the idea of living by the park caught on, the price of the building land shot up to 11/4d a yard in the years between 1842 to 1845. The ratepayers must have been very grateful. The sale of the building plots from time to time took care of the financial costs of the construction and maintenance of the park.[1]

Paxton's plan allowed for about 800 houses. Eleven terraces are shown and fifty-four villas. In addition there were two crescents, perhaps in imitation of the Regent's Park idea, and other terraces to the south and west of the park beyond the surrounding roads. The plan was left to evolve. The crescents and terraces as shown on the plan did not materialise. Many of the villas were built in the manner set out though some are semi-detached and not detached as designated, and there are terraces though short ones.

The architectural quality varies. It has been suggested that the best houses were built before the 1860s. Some of the most expensive houses were built along Ashville Road.

Paxton laid down principles rather than specific details. The buildings were to relate to the formation of the landscape and blend in. The houses were to be seen from varying points of view in attractive and changing relationships to each other and to the planting. He wanted them to enhance the view from the park as they peeped through their leaves. Their gardens would reflect back and continue the image of the park. Each owner or tenant was to have the illusion that he was surrounded by his own parkland to which he would have direct access via a rear gate in his garden.

Only the very best materials were to be used for the houses and they were to have thick walls. The fronts were to be of Storeton stone or red or yellow brick.

The building of the houses around the park was carried on over a number of years. This is why it is unlikely that Joseph Paxton himself supervised it. Not all the sites were taken up. Consider the vacant plots that lie between the carriageways and the public roads. Occasionally the building land has been given over to other uses.

Cannon Hill in Park Road West is thought to have accorded with Paxton's idea. This terrace with its symmetrical Italianate facade, was so named because of two cannons from the Crimean War which stood nearby. Within living memory they were to be found one on each side of the 'Logan' stone. Cannon Hill Terrace and Cannon Mount were recently magnificently restored by Merseyside Improved Houses, even to the ornamental balcony railings. They are no longer single family units but flats, as are 90 and 92 Park Road South, also restored by M.I.H.[2] Previously these buildings were in a sad state of decay. Neighbouring 'Abbot's Grange', has tiles in the vestibule from the Della Robbia pottery and also some fine stained glass. Nearby, new flats have been built on the site of a large pair of yellow brick houses demolished some years ago.

1. The land cost	£69,690
Legal costs were	£540
Interest 7 years	£23,796
Planting etc.	£9,280
	£103,306

Cost of drainage, excavation and planting amounted to nearly £70,000 but the building land enhanced its value and became worth about 7 times its original cost.

2. Rumour would have it that 90 and 92 Park Road South once stood in the vicinity of Monks' ferry and that the owner could have been Joseph Harrison, a Liverpool merchant who was a pioneer settler in Birkenhead buying land for building purposes in 1820. The houses were removed to the present site following the Shipyard development of the mid-1820s when the residential amenities of the riverside sharply declined. This fascinating idea lacks proof. The architecture is supposed to date the houses not earlier than the 1840s. They are shown in their present position on the 1858 map.

7. THE PARK IS OPENED

Birkenhead Park was opened to the public by Lord Morpeth.[1] He had opened Morpeth Dock on the same day. It was Easter Monday, 5th April, 1847. William and John Laird were present and many of the Town Commissioners. William Potter was at that time their chairman. Although the park had been available to the public for some months before the official ceremony, a crowd of 56,000 had assembled on the day. The 'Liverpool Mercury' informed its readers that the fair sex was well represented.

Speeches were made and 'rural sports' held on the eastern side of the park. Lord Morpeth walked around commenting on various aspects of the park and then 'ascended an eminence' near to the lake and planted a tree. He informed the spectators that he himself was a keen gardener. The new park must have looked very beautiful with its gently picturesque landscaping, its broad open areas for cricket and archery and its more densely planted part. The giant rockery at the western end of the lake in the Lower Park was a joy to the eye. Newspaper reports tell us that flags were everywhere; that it was fine and warm and nature was doing her best to make the day a success. The graceful swans on the lakes were much admired.

OPENING
OF
BIRKENHEAD DOCKS
PARK, &c.

1847 **RURAL** *1847*

SPORTS
WILL TAKE PLACE
IN BIRKENHEAD PARK,
On Monday next, April 5,

UNDER THE MANAGEMENT OF THE FOLLOWING COMMITTEE:—

MR. WILLIAM CRAVEN, CHAIRMAN.

Mr ROBERT HUGHES	Mr WILLIAM WALKER
„ WALTER WALKER	„ J. MORRIS
„ HUGH WILLIAMS	„ JOHN GRAHAM
„ J. BOYLE	„ RICHARD DEVALVE
„ WILLIAM RIMMER	„ JOHN McGIVERING
„ CHARLES PADLEY	„ J. MORRISON
„ THOMAS HILTON	„ JOHN FRITH
„ THOMAS WALLEY	„ JAMES HUME
„ JOHN HILTON	

UMPIRES:—Mr. J. HILTON, Mr. J. BOYLE, and Mr. R. HUGHES.

THE SPORTS WILL COMMENCE WITH

THREE SACK RACES

The First for a Prize of 10s.; the Second, for Young Men under 21 years of age, for 10s.; the Third, for defeated Candidates, for 7s. 6d.

A HURDLE RACE—Prizes, 10s. for the First, & 5s for the 2nd man

A FOOT RACE, open to all the World, first in to receive 10s.; second. 5s.

THREE GREASY POLES will be fixed in different parts of the Park, with Good Hats and Baragon Coats on the top for the successful Competitors.

A FOOT RACE FOR WOMEN OF ALL AGES,

Open to all the World: Fifteen Shilling: for the First, and Five Shillings for the Second best.

A PIG CHASE, VALUE TWO POUNDS, WITH ITS TAIL SOAPED.

No Sawdust, Sand or Pitch allowed. Entrance, 1s. each—not more than twenty to enter.

A DONKEY RACE.

10s. for the Last, and 5s. for the Last but one. ☞ No Owner to ride his own Donkey, and no Carrots allowed.

A BLIND-FOLDED WHEELBARROW RACE!

Ten Shillings for the First, and Five Shillings for the Second.

A BELL RACE FOR A NEW HAT.

Not more than eight to start.

A Grinning Match, through Six Horse Collars,

The tallest may to have Five Shillings.

THREE BASINS OF HOT STIRRAH

To be eaten by lads not exceeding 16 years of age, for Five Shillings. No Timoh allowed.

The Sports will commence at Two o'clock precisely, and no Person will be allowed to enter for any of the Prizes without a Ticket from the Committee.

R. M. HOGAN, Clerk of the Course.
GEORGE POWELL, Secretary.

☞ ALL DOGS FOUND IN THE PARK WILL BE DESTROYED.

THE GRAND
DISPLAY OF FIRE WORKS

Will take place at .... the Dock Quays.

The pedestrians, as they crowded along Conway Street, could buy oranges and nuts from street vendors and apparatus for taking part in the games. In the afternoon bands paraded. Tents were pitched and 'creature comforts' sold. A favourite was hot stir-up, a porridge-like mixture.

From an early hour workmen had been busy preparing stages and poles and hurdles, etc. The men on the committee were kept hard at work getting sacks ready, greasing poles and shaving pigs and soaping their tails.

All the proceedings of the afternoon began punctually. There were eleven contests altogether including a donkey race — no carrots allowed! This race operated on the same principle as a slow-bike race, the object being to be last! Each rider had to ensure that his neighbour's mount was first past the winning post. The spectators found it hilarious. The dense crowds became very animated. The rider of the last donkey received ten-shillings and the next to last, five-shillings. No mean sums in 1847. Ten-shillings was also paid to the winner of the 'cleverly won' Hurdle race and to the winner of the foot-race, second prize again being five-shillings. There was a race for men of all ages and a race for the ladies. There was much merriment over the climbing of the two greased poles. The man who won the contest involving catching a shaved pig with a greasy tail, did so by catching hold of its leg and holding its tail in his mouth! In the 'blindfolded' wheelbarrow race, the contestants started together and had to reach a given point. There was 'a bell race for a new hat' and a competition called gurning through the horse's collar which involved hideously distorting the face. Three lads happily took part in a race to eat three basins full of stir-up, the winner pocketing five-shillings.

The weather of the 1840s being no more predictable than that of our day it became cloudy during the latter part of the afternoon and showered at intervals. Lord Morpeth left the proceedings shortly after 5 o'clock to catch the ferry prior to returning to London.

That night there was a firework display at Morpeth Dock. It had been a day for Birkonians to remember.

Birkenhead Park became very famous. It attracted visitors from all over the world. One of these, in 1850, was a man called F.L. Olmsted. Mr. Olmsted, who re-visited the park in 1858, was particularly impressed by the circulation pattern. He was to design the Central Park in New York. He drew his inspiration from our park here in Birkenhead.[2]

The Victorians, with their zeal for reform, did not lose their enthusiasm for creating new parks.

Joseph Paxton adapted to changing fashion in his later work. His vision of an eighteenth century landscape park gave way to the more formal Victorian public park layout.

---

1. George William Frederick Howard, (1802-1864), 7th Earl of Carlisle, (Viscount Morpeth), was a prominent member of the Government. Amongst his appointments, he was the Chief Commissioner of Woods and Forests, under Lord Russell, from 1846 to 1850. He was also a writer and published poems, etc.

2. See page 41

8. LEISURE-TIME PURSUITS

Today we take it for granted that parks are dual-purpose. The idea that they should be used for other forms of recreation other than 'promenading', was a revolutionary one when Paxton designed Birkenhead Park. He deliberately set aside areas for the playing of games. Perhaps he foresaw that time for leisure pursuits would increase. He realised that the playing of games would enhance the view against the back-cloth of trees.

Birkenhead Park Cricket Club is as old as the park itself. The Club's grounds in the Lower Park were once the scene of a very famous match when they challenged an All England XI. The match took place on three days in June 1869. The ground was roped round with red and green bunting. The weather was perfect. People from Oxton and Claughton flocked to watch. The women wore pretty summer dresses and carried parasols. Men from the Britannia Works and Laird's Yard were given an extra half-day holiday in honour of the match. The result was a draw. England needed only 17 runs to win when the players had to rush off to catch their train!

Another well-known Cricket Club in the Lower Park is St. Mary's, established in 1878. It was originally affiliated to St. Mary's Parish Church. Early presidents of the Club were Ministers of the Church.[1]

In 1896 the question of allowing cricket in the Upper Park was considered but it was thought that the cost of levelling the uneven ground was too great and it would interfere with the land drains.

Birkenhead Park is famous for its Rugby Club which came to the Upper Park in 1886. In 1919 one of 'Park's' well-known players, James Baxter, started the fund to purchase the ground as a memorial to no less than 75 members of the Club who had been killed in the Great War. In the 2nd World War the grounds of the Club suffered badly from land mines.

Although bowls and tennis are now the only other surviving games, the park has also hosted archery, skittles, putting, quoiting, curling, skating and cycle racing.[2] Hockey and netball have also been played within the confines of school playing fields within the park.

In our day we do not see strings of saddle horses and harness horses brought for their daily exercise. Modern children are rarely accompanied by nursery governesses and nursemaids, but they enjoy feeding the water fowl just as much as did their counterparts of the last century. At that time, coots, water hens and dab chicks abounded in the bush covered banks and grassy spaces near to the lakes. There were wild rabbits too. Until recently rabbits could still be seen on the island in the Upper Park. The virus disease, myxomatosis, took its toll and at other times, when the lake has silted in places, foxes may have gone over to the island. Drakes, ducks, Canadian and Chinese geese, swans, shell-drake, muscovy, decoy ducks, teal and mallards used the lakes. The swans were reported to have died of neglect in the 1st World War. Today we do not see so great a variety though there are Canada geese, moorhens and mallards.

Every kind of coarse fish except pike used to be stocked. There would be carp, dace, rudd, bream, perch and eels, roach and tench. Fishermen had to observe strict rules about what could be caught and when. The water was kept clean by park-keepers and gardeners who had a long, shallow-bottomed green boat which they propelled with a long pole.

Many creatures have been donated to the park. On Friday, 17th October, 1845, John Feilden of Mollington Hall, presented a pair of swans. A gift of 5 Muscovy ducks were received from the Braden Dairy Company of Birkenhead in 1898. A Mr. Lilwall's offer of 6 squirrels was accepted in 1908. Red and grey squirrels have been seen in recent times. In 1915 a pony complete with cart was introduced. This was to help with mowing and carting. In 1919 the Park's Superintendent bought a horse.

In the days before radio and television and the cinema, coming to listen to the band was a very popular pastime. In the years between 1894 and the start of the 1st War, no less that fifteen bands were taking turns to play in the park.[3] The bands played on weeknights as well as at the weekends. Concerts on Sundays would be strictly devoted to 'sacred' music. In 1906 a payment of £2.10/- was made for each performance if 20 bandsmen were present. If this number could not be mustered, then the fee was £2. The performance would take place regardless of the weather. The programme had to be submitted to the Parks' Superintendent for approval and then would go the press for publication. Summer evening concerts would last from 7.30 p.m. to 9.30 p.m.

Paxton's bandstand had doubled as a boathouse. The shell only remains. The balustrading and pantile roof has gone. Another bandstand existed, also in the Lower Park. This was in the vicinity of the 'Logan' stone and in the direction of Cannon Mount. A further bandstand, a short distance away, by the approach path to the lake, fell victim to enemy action in the 2nd World War. Bands then took to using a widened area of the footpath in the re-opened Upper Park.

The bandstands had been used for other forms of entertainment. Every Whit Monday and occasionally on August Bank Holidays, the poor children from Charles Thompson's Mission would give open-air concerts and collect for their funds. During the Great War the Misses Bell of Birkenhead held open-air concerts in aid of local war funds.

The Birkenhead and District Temperance Federation and Band of Hope Union's Annual Children's Day Demonstrations were held in the park. International Champion Gymnasts under the auspices of the Y.M.C.A. gave displays.

The Boys' Brigade has used the park for parades when the bugle band will perform.

The park has been used for sponsored walks.

An event of very special note took place in 1917. The Royal National Eisteddfod of Wales was held in the month of September. A pavilion was erected to accommodate 10,000 people. A reminder of this great occasion is the 'Logan' stone left behind to commemorate the event.[4]

---

1. See Appendix 'C'.

2. See Appendix 'D'.

3. See Appendix 'A'.

4. This stone, which is in the Lower Park not far from Cannon Hill, was donated by a Welshman, a Birkenhead town councillor — David Evans. Councillor Evans, and his sons, built most of the houses on Park Road North and the avenues running off it. In the present day, his grandson, Lord Evans of Claughton, has a keen interest in the well-being of the park.

28

Lydia Fitzpatrick is well known for her attractive drawings and paintings of local scenes. Among the most interesting features of Birkenhead Park are the park lodges, each entirely different, but each a brilliant example of a particular building style. Although Lydia has made previous drawings of the lodges the illustrations on the following pages have been drawn especially for this book. The front cover illustration is also reproduced from an original water colour of hers.

The Grand Entrance Gateway, Junction of Park Road North and Park Road East.

The Castellated Lodge. Park Road West.

The Norman Lodges - East and West. Park Road North neighbouring Norman Street.

The Italian Lodge. Park Road South.

33

The Gothic Lodge. Junction of Park Road East and Park Road South.

The Central Lodge. Ashville Road.

9. ECHOING ENGLAND'S HISTORY

The history of our country has been reflected by activities held within the park. Not long after the park had been opened England had been in fear of an invasion by the forces of Napoleon III. The Cheshire Volunteer Movement had been formed. Birkonians flocked to watch them drilling in the park and to see their parades and field days. Successive generations of the Volunteers made use of the park for inspections and reviews. In 1906 the Birkenhead Royal Naval Volunteers carried out drill there too. In 1907 they held a field gun competition.

In 1913 the Ceremonial Parade of the Cheshire Field Company, Royal Engineers, was held in the Upper Park.

In both world wars the park played its role. In the 1st War areas of the Upper Park were given over to sheep grazing and the growing of vegetables. Sheep were not a new feature. Mr. Olmsted, the designer of New York's Central Park, had commented on sheep being there in 1850. The sheep reinforced the idea of a pastoral landscape. In 1896, Mr. John Evans Junior of Birkenhead was paying £15 a year for pasturage in the Upper Park. In 1899 Mr. D. Whiteway of Birkenhead took over but had to pay the £15 in two half-yearly instalments.

In the 2nd World War the Upper Park was used for allotments.

In 1951 the Festival of Britain, marking the Centenary of the Great Exhibition of 1851, was celebrated with displays and parades in Birkenhead Park Rugby Ground. John Arlott, the Commentator, was present.

Various royal events have been celebrated by Birkonians with sports and games and displays. Queen Victoria's Diamond Jubilee in 1897 must have been a great occasion. Platforms were erected at the Park Entrance and in the Upper Park. The park was closed on 18th June, 1897 and there was a charge for admission to watch the events. Refreshment tents were erected. The total cost of the occasion was not more than £60. The proceeds went to aid local hospitals. Festivities were held on the occasion of Edward VII's coronation in 1902.

The accession of our sovereigns has been reflected in tree planting. Oak trees mark the coronations of Edward VII, George V, and George VI. No plaques now single out these trees. One is situated near to the Junior Department of Park High School in the Upper Park. It stands in a solitary position. A group of trees near to the 'Logan' stone in the Lower Park have all been especially planted to mark events. On the accession of Elizabeth II an avenue of lime trees was planted by school children in the Lower Park.

10. REFLECTIONS TODAY

Birkenhead Park was considered to be Joseph Paxton's finest achievement in landscape architecture. It is numbered amongst the top six world-famous parks. The others are the Bois de Boulogne in France; the Central Park in New York; the Friedrich-Wilhelmsgarten in Germany; the Botanic Gardens in Melbourne, and Akahi Park in Kobe, Japan.

Next time you visit Birkenhead Park walk around the lakes. Look at the scene with fresh eyes. Try to shut out the railings. Visualise it as it must have been 100 and more years ago. It still looks like countryside miraculously preserved in the heart of Birkenhead. It is still very beautiful. Sadly the conservatory, once a riot of colour with many exotic plants and cacti, is no more.[1] You can no longer stand on the Swiss bridge and enjoy the various views of the lake and see the reflections mirrored in the water. Nevertheless much remains. Whether it be the banks of Spring daffodils or the crimson and ochre tints of Autumn foliage or a lakeside seat on a sunny day, the park provides for the needs of the modern town dweller.

Even Sir William Jackson could not have foreseen how Birkenhead was to grow, swallowing up other districts as it did so. The 110 inhabitants of 1801 had multiplied up to 99,857 by 1891. In 1968 Birkenhead numbered 141,950. Although the tide of urban population is now ebbing away from inner areas, our town bears no relation to that of Sir William Jackson's day. Very few will have even heard his name. But to him, his fellow Town Commissioners, and to Sir Joseph Paxton, many generations of Birkonians owe their very grateful thanks.

Thurstaston Common was acquired for the town in 1881. In 1885, 21 acres were opened in Mersey Park. Victoria Park was added in 1901 and Bidston Hill in the years between 1894 and 1908. The Arno was opened in 1912. Arrowe Park, with its 425 acres was acquired for the town in 1927.

---

1. This stood on the site of the palmhouse still remembered by many.

FROM GLYN HOLDEN'S POSTCARD COLLECTION

38

FROM GLYN HOLDEN'S POSTCARD COLLECTION

39

Swiss Bridge, Birkenhead Park.

FROM GLYN HOLDEN'S POSTCARD COLLECTION

8240   View in Park.   Birkenhead.

40

When the park was opened on April 5th, 1847, "The Stranger's Guide" attempted to imagine the scene and depict it.

> "We have not progressed far ere we come to a beautifully constructed rustic bridge thrown over a portion of a large meandering clear lake. This bridge connects an island with the mainland and as we proceed along the walks of the island on the margin of the lake our attention is excited by the stately sailing of majestic snow white swans up and down the stream. On the right there is a small ornamental building which juts a short way into the water beneath which is a boat house containing a canoe. The building was designed for the accommodation of a band of musicians but it is to be regretted that hitherto the ears of the admiring frequenters of these gardens have not been saluted with melodious sounds . . . At the end of the lake we perceive a rockery from which the admirable manner in which it has been erected has often given rise to the question whether it is natural or artificial. The great variety of rock plants which spring from the crevices delight the eye of the cursory spectator and interest for hours the lover of botanical science."

Quoted in "The Park and the Town" by George F. Chadwick. Page 69.

The following extract is from and eye-witness account of how the park appeared to F.L. Olmsted when he visited it in 1850. Birkenhead Park during these early years was attracting many visitors. Mr. Olmsted, the architect of Central Park, New York, drew on the layout of Birkenhead Park for inspiration. This was his impression of the visit.

> "The gateway, which is about a mile and a half from the ferry and quite back of the town is a great massive block of handsome Ionic architecture, standing alone, and unsupported by anything else in the vicinity, and looking as I think, heavy and awkward . . . The ground immediately within the grand entrance is very simple . . . There is a large archway for carriages and two smaller ones for those on foot, and on either side, and over these, are rooms which probably serve as convenient lodges for the labourers. No porter appears and the gates are freely open to the public.

"Walking a short distance up an avenue we passed through another light iron gate into a thick, luxuriant and diversified garden ... Gardening here has reached a perfection that I have never before dreamed of ... We passed by winding paths over acres and acres with a constant varying surface, where on all sides were growing every variety of shrubs and flowers all set in orders of greenest closest turf and all kept with most consummate neatness. At a distance of a quarter of a mile from the gate we came to an open field of clean bright green sward, closely mown, on which a large tent was pitched and a party of boys and a party of gentlemen in another part were playing cricket. Beyond this was a large meadow with rich groups of trees under which a flock of sheep were reposing and girls and women with children were playing. We were threatened with a shower and we hastened back to look for shelter which we found in a pagoda on an island approached by a Chinese bridge. It was soon filled, as were the other ornamental buildings, by a crowd of those who like ourselves had been overtaken by the rain and I was glad to observe that all the privileges of the garden were enjoyed about equally by all classes. There were some who were attended by servants, and sent at once for their carriages, but a large proportion were of the common ranks and a few women with children or suffering from ill-health were evidently the wives of very humble labourers. There were a number of strangers, and some were observed with note books and portfolios, that seemed to have come from a distance. The summer houses, lodges, bridges, etc. were all well-constructed and of undecaying materials. One of the bridges which we crossed was of our countryman, Remington's patent, an extremely light and graceful erection.

"But this is but a small part. Besides the cricket and archery grounds, large valleys were made verdant, extensive drives arranged, plantations, clumps and avenues of trees formed, and a large park laid out and all this magnificent pleasure ground is entirely, unreservedly and forever the people's own."

This extract quoted by Chadwick. op. cit. Page 71, was from "Walks and Talks of an American Farmer in England" by F.L. Olmsted.

Mrs. Hilda Gamlin, the Birkenhead authoress, was drawing on her memories when she wrote the following in 1892.

"To these hillocks children would bring baskets of Pace eggs on Easter Monday. Wickets were fixed at intervals at the foot of the 'bonks' when the children took their eggs to the top of the hills and rolled them down, aiming to pass them unbroken between the wickets. Prizes were offered for the two youngsters who displayed the most skill in the rolling and for the ones who brought the largest assortment of decorated eggs... Large crowds of children and adults watched. It was followed by an Easter Day Dance performed by the youngsters who were then given buns to eat."

"... The space of ground near Birkenhead, now called the park, was a short time ago, like much suburban land near the metropolis, a mere marsh, over which thick mists hung at nightfall. It was thoroughly drained by Sir Joseph Paxton, with drains varying in depth from seven feet to close surface drains. The mists and fogs created on this tract have, since the drains came into operation, disappeared . . ."

from 'the Drainage of Parks and Suburban Land' published by the Board of Health 'Minutes of Information'. Jan 1852.

Quoted by Chadwick in 'The Works of Sir Joseph Paxton'. Page 203.

SIR JOSEPH PAXTON, Bart, was born on August 3rd, 1803 at Milton Bryan, near Woburn. He was the seventh son of a Bedfordshire farmer. When he was fifteen he obtained employment as a garden boy at a local house, Battlesden. His special abilities soon manifested and by 1826 he was head gardener to the 6th Duke of Devonshire at Chatsworth House in Derbyshire. He married the house-keeper's niece, Sarah Brown, in January 1827. She was a great support to him in his work. His responsibilities to the Duke grew to include matters of management of the whole estate. With the encouragement of the Duke he began to travel widely to gain experience.

Paxton's list of accomplishments are formidable. He was a landscape gardener, a botanist and horticulturalist, and an architect. A designer of public parks and suburbs and of conventional buildings, he also built glass structures for more than twenty years before he designed the Crystal Palace. He had business interests and was a railway speculator. He was also a journalist and a Member of Parliament. He had to resign his seat in early 1865 due to over work and ill-health. He died a few months later on the 8th June. Like his former much-respected employer, the 6th Duke, Paxton was buried at Edensor, on the Chatsworth estate.

SIR WILLIAM JACKSON, Bart, was born at Warrington on the 28th April, 1805. He was the seventh son of his father, Peter, also a seventh son.

Sir William was a Liverpool tradesman. His business was on the west side of Church Street between Paradise Street and St. Peter's Church. He became a successful shipowner and merchant and a large employer of labour.

In 1824 William Laird — with his brother John,, established his boiler-making and shipbuilding yard on the margin of Wallasey Pool. William Jackson, and his brother, John Somerville Jackson, became prominent in the affairs of the new town and in promoting its development. In 1846, he retired from the Birkenhead Commissioners to become M.P. for the North Derbyshire constituency of Newcastle-under-Lyme. That same year he moved from his Hamilton Square home to the newly built Manor House in Claughton.

Sir William was a Liberal. He finally lost his North Derbyshire seat in 1868.

Later in life he did not live in Birkenhead. He died at his home in Portland Place, London on 31st January, 1876 in his 71st year after a protracted illness. His wife, Lady Jackson had died a year earlier on 25th January, 1875.

Sir William Jackson was buried at Flaybrick Hill Cemetery in Birkenhead.

APPENDIX 'A'

Bands mentioned as performing in Birkenhead Park between the years 1894 and 1916.*

Birkenhead Mission Band.

Hope Jones Electric Organ Band.

Birkenhead Borough Brass Band. (Later named Birkenhead Borough Prize Band).

Boys' Band of Kirkdale Children's Charity.

Birkenhead Shore Road Station Brass Band.

Tranmere Gleam Silver Prize Band.

London and North Western Employees Brass Band.

Regimental Band, The Cheshire Regiment. 1st Battalion.

Birkenhead and District Postal Band.

Port Sunlight Prize Band.

Royal Artillery Mounted Band.

Birkenhead Protestant Brass Band.

The Bromborough Pool Brass Band.

Albert Memorial Industrial Schoolboys' Band.

Liverpool Workshops for the Blind Band.

When the new bandstand was opened in the park on the 15th/16th June 1929 there was a programme of music by Irwell Springs (Bacup) Band during the afternoon and evening on the 15th. On the 16th, the Liverpool City Police Band under the Chief Inspector gave a performance.

---

* Birkenhead Parks and Cemeteries Committee Minutes —
  Books commencing 1891 (6): 1905 (8): 1912 (10).

APPENDIX 'B'

Football teams mentioned as playing in Birkenhead Park between the years 1894 and 1922.*

St. Edward's Rugby Football Club.
Brassey Street Mission Rugby Football Club.
The Claughton Rugby Football Club.
White Rose Rugby Football Club.
Holy Trinity Football Club.
Birkenhead Park Football Club.
St. Nathaniel's Football Club.
G.F. Milnes & Co. Carriage Works Football Club.
1st Volunteers Battalion, The Cheshire Regiment, Football Club.
The Sports Committee of Birkenhead Teachers' Association arranged for scholars belonging to Elementary Schools to have facilities.
Brunswick Rugby Football Club.
Prenton Football Club.
Borough Road Mission Football Club.
Birkenhead Old Boys Football Club.
Higher Elementary Council School.
Lowe Street Wesleyan Football Club.
Boys' Brigade.
Mount Junior Football Club.
Shaftesbury Boys Club.
National Assoc. of Discharged & Demobilized Sailors and Soldiers.
Clover, Clayton Football Club.
St. Laurence's Football Club.
Grange Football Club.
Hemingford Street Old Boys.
St. Peter's.
St. Mary's and Tranmere Boys Club.
Birkenhead Melville Football Club.
British Legion.
Glenville Football Club.
Our Lady's Football Club.
St. Anne's Football Club.
Stokeville Football Club.

During the years of the Great War the lists of teams denoted as using the football grounds were noticeably those of boys' teams.

---

* Ibid. plus book commencing 1918 (11).

APPENDIX 'C'

Cricket Clubs mentioned as playing in Birkenhead Park between the years 1893 and 1921.*

Birkenhead Police Athletic Club.
Birkenhead St. Mary's Cricket Club.
St. John's Working Lads Cricket Club.
St. Peter's Cricket Club.
St. Edward's Cricket Club.
St. Matthew's Cricket Club.
The Cheshire Lines Cricket Club.
St. Paul's Boys' Cricket Club.
United Methodist Cricket Club.
Brassey Street Cricket Club. (The Mission).
Grosvenor Cricket Club.
St. Andrew's Cricket Club.
The Birkenhead Railways Cricket Club.
Cedar Cricket Club.
General Post Office Cricket Club.
St. Aidan's Cricket Club.
Ravenscroft Cricket Club.
Birkenhead Primrose Cricket Club.
Birkenhead Borough Cricket Club.
St. John's Bible Class Cricket Club.
Conway Cricket Club.
Corporation Tramways and Municipal Employees Cricket Club.
Lowe Street Wesleyan Cricket Club.
Claughton Victoria Cricket Club.
Elementary Schools.
Birkenhead Parish Church Cricket Club.
Brunswick Wesleyan Cricket Club.
Y.M.C.A.
Birkenhead Institute.
Birkenhead Boys Brigade.
Shaftesbury Boys' Cricket Club.

During the years of the Great War the lists of Clubs denoted as being allocated grounds in Birkenhead Park were noticeably those of Boys Clubs.

---

* Ibid.

APPENDIX 'D'

Wages and Prices current in the years between 1893 and 1919.*

1893 — 12 extra labourers were employed at 3/- per day to repair the drives. (The aim was to provide work for the unemployed).

1894 — The labourers had a rise of 2d per day.
— Mr. William Spann, the park keeper, resplendent in his £5 uniform, blue uniform coat and trousers, scarlet vest and cap with cover — was earning 20/- per week.

1899 — Articles of uniform were ordered for the park watchmen.
2 frock coats at 44/9d each.
2 scarlet vests at 11/6d each.
2 pairs cloth trousers at 16/9d per pair.
2 caps and covers at 4/6d each.

1906 — Boots for park keepers cost 11/6d per pair.

1906 — The Parks' Superintendent reported on the question of granting a week's holiday to Corporation workmen. In the case of the parks the total cost involved was £14.

— The Parks' Superintendent received a rise bringing his salary up to £220 per annum. (When Mr. W. Parkinson had been appointed in 1886 his salary had been £100 per annum).

1907 — The minimum wage for all able-bodied workmen was to be 24/- per week.

* * * * *

1895 — Best red Jersey Gravel (200-tons) for the footpaths was ordered at 6/9d per ton.

1896 — Penmaenmawr Macadam (1¼") — 200-tons was ordered for repairing the carriage drives at 8/3d per ton.
(In 1914 it was considered that the park drives should be closed to motor traffic failing which the Local Government Board should be asked to sanction a bye-law fixing the maximum speed at 7 m.p.h.).

* * * * *

1895 — On the 13th May a youth was apprehended by P.C. No. 98 Brown whilst off duty, for damaging the railings in Birkenhead Park. A gratuity of 5/- was paid to P.C. Brown by the Parks' Superintendent for 'vigilance displayed by him whilst off duty.'

1896 — Printing and supplying 400 copies of Birkenhead Park Byelaws in sheet form cost £1.8/-.

Painting the seats in Birkenhead and Mersey Parks cost £10.10/-. Painting and varnishing the bandstand in Birkenhead park cost £8.

1906 — 48 pairs of ivory mounted bowls, properly engraved — were purchased at 9/6 a pair and 24 jacks at 2/- each.

— 2 new rows of boxes in the bowls house for the new equipment were made at a cost of £1.10/-

— A shelter erected in the Recreation Grounds cost £45.

1908 — New conveniences and a drinking fountain in Upper Park — £290.

— Rental of Refreshment Rooms £15 per annum.

1919 — The Parks' Superintendent purchased a horse for £48.

* * * * *

In 1898 a season ticket for bowls would cost 5/-. (The Curator of the recreation grounds could prohibit anyone playing whom he felt to be in an 'unfit condition.')

In 1897 when the skittle alley was in a dilapidated condition it was decided to remove it and put a quoiting rink in its place. Two years later the idea of converting the quoiting rinks into an additional bowling green was considered. In 1905 the park's new bowling green cost £122. In 1908 an additional bowling green and 3 quoiting pitches were prepared to adjoin the existing greens. £150 was allocated for this. 24 pairs of quoits and 24 pairs of bowls and 15 jacks were ordered for these new greens and grounds. They cost £25. In 1913 it was decided that rubber overshoes should be worn by persons using the greens and 200 pairs were purchased at 2/4d a pair. The charge to the public for the compulsory use of these overshoes was ½d. In 1915, a year after the opening of the new Recreation Ground, it was decided to allow wounded soldiers from the Borough Hospital the free use of the bowling greens.

1908 had seen alterations to the archery grounds in Park Road East. They were to be used for a recreation ground for Borough Secondary Schools.

Mr. Samuel Coathup was the curator of the Recreation Grounds for many years. His salary was 21/- a week though in 1896 he received an increase of 1/- a week. On his resignation in 1907, his successor, Mr. W. Wood, took over at a wage of 30/- a week.

Receipts from the Recreation Grounds were calculated on a 2 or 3 weeks basis. In the mid-1890s receipts during April and May would range from £1.15/- to £2.5/-. In early August they would have risen to £5.10/- and £6.5/-, but then would fall away again to 15/- to £1.5/- in late September and early October when the recreation grounds would be closed for the winter.

In 1905 £80 was spent on repairs and alterations to the Refreshment rooms. Councillor Russell suggested that the Committee should under the terms of 'The Unemployed Workmen's Act of 1905' ask the Distress Committee to make a grant towards the cost of the work. This method of financing work undertaken in the park was again used in 1932. Various works were put in hand and applications were made to the Unemployment Grants Committee for assistance towards the cost involved.

In June 1914 a new Curator of the Tennis Courts was appointed. It was a Mr. W.J. Morris whose salary was 30/- a week.

In June 1889 tickets for fishing cost 10/6d for a year. Non-householders and non-ratepayers paid £1.1s.

On the 21st January 1907 a thousand perch were obtained from Mr. J. Walker of Bowness, Windermere, at a cost of £5 and 200 Bream from the Manor Fishery, Caistor, Lincolnshire, at a cost of £2.

---

* Ibid.

APPENDIX 'E'

Rules when fishing in the park lakes.*

No person was allowed to use more than one rod at the same time or to use side or night lines. The penalty would be to lose his ticket.

The close season, from 15th May to 15th June, meant no fishing except for trout between the hours of 9 and 4 and not later than 9 p.m. and not at all on Sundays. All fish caught in the lakes of less than the following weights had to be returned alive to the waters:-

Carp and Tench	½-lb.
Perch	5-oz.
Roach and Rudd	4-oz.

except in the case for Rudd required for live bait purposes. Any trout less than 9 inches in length or which was caught between the 1st October and 1st March, had to be immediately returned alive to the waters.

---

* "Laws Re Fishing in Park Lakes" — 1889.

APPENDIX 'F'

The following is from a 1967 Victorian Society list of buildings on the park perimeter that it wished to see preserved:-

*A.   All entrance lodges and original park buildings.
       i.e. Main Entrance; Castellated Lodge; Central Lodge; Gothic Lodge; Italian Lodge; North Lodges East and West. Boat House; Cast Iron Bridge; Swiss Bridge.

A	1	Ashville Road.
*C	15 and 17	- " -
*C	19 and 21	- " -
*A	57	- " -
*A	59 and 61	- " -
*B	8	- " -
*A	10	- " -
*B	12 and 14	- " -
*A	16	- " -
*A	1	Cavendish Road.
*B	2 and 3	- " -
*B	4 and 5	- " -
*A	Royden House	Park Road North.
A	2	Park Road South
B	8 and 10	- " -
B	12 and 14	- " -
B	16 and 18	- " -
*A	90 and 92	- " -
*C	94	- " -
*C	96 and 98	- " -
*A	Cannon Hill	Park Road West
*C	2 and 4 and 6	- " -
*C	8	- " -

* * * * *

KEY

*   Buildings of importance on account of their group value and relationship to the landscape.

A   Buildings of architectural importance which should certainly be preserved.

B   Lesser architectural importance but desirable to preserve.

C   Little or no architectural importance but which because of the importance of their group value and relationship to the landscape should be replaced only with caution.

* * * * *

Memorandum of Birkenhead Park — Victorian Society — Architectural Review — April 1967.

APPENDIX 'G'

The following extracts are from the notes made by Mr. Edward Hubbard, then of the Victorian Society, for a Birkenhead Park Walkabout with members of the Birkenhead History Society on 28th July, 1973. (Revised May 1975).

* * * * *

"Unless otherwise stated, the examples of the perimeter housing referred to,date from immediately or shortly after the completion of the Park, i.e. late 1840s or early 1850s.

Main Entrance. *A monumental structure of U-plan, with a pair of tall lodges linked by a triple-arcaded screen. Giant order of unfluted Ionic pilasters to the lodges. Entablature and superstructure of screen break forward above the columns. Elaborate scroll-like ornament above the centre. The application of the order gives a sense of mass and solidity, and links the three parts together as a unified composition. In Park Road North, a large classical semi-detached block now known as* Royden House.

Lower lake Boathouse. *Strategically sited to form a feature from several viewpoints. Pilastered and arcaded upper storey intended as a bandstand. Original balustrading and pantile roof have gone. . . . the* Swiss Bridge . . . *a delightful covered timber structure of the greatest value within the landscape.*

Gothic Lodge. *Neo-Elizabethan. Less attractive than the others, but equally important as contributing to the stylistic variety and having links with Paxton/Robertson work elsewhere. Nearby, in* Park Road South, *some pleasant houses, particularly* No. 2. *Late 1850s or early 1860s. Unusually pure classical for so late a date.* Nos. 8-18. *Three semi-detached Gothic blocks, probably of similar date.*

Much of the open area of the Lower Park has suffered from inappropriate later structures and alterations, including a straight avenue. Italian Lodge. *An excellent composition of single and two-storey blocks revolving around a belvedere tower. Almost a miniature beau ideal of the Loudonish Italianate villa. Detailing of the greatest sensitivity and refinements.* Nos. 90-92, Park

54

Road South . . . *restrainedly classical. Not stucco-faced, but ashlar . . . Groups with* Cannon Hill, *Park Road West. Late 1850s or early 1860s. One of the two terraces built and the only one of real architectural or group value. Its symmetrical Italianate facade forms a feature in the landscape of the greatest importance.*

At the south end of Ashville Road *a group of villas which, of all parts of the perimeter housing, most closely approximate to Paxton's original plan. The houses are probably by the local architect, Walter Scott.* Nos. 59-61 *Two large semi-detached houses, though asymmetrical. Jacobethan style.* No. 57. *A splendid little villa. Irregular grouping, but Jacobethan style, with quite heavy ornament.* No. 8. *Brick Gothic harmed by large extensions of the 1890s.* No. 10. *Attractive but thin Gothic, providing a reminder of how far removed from the contemporary world of Pugin and ecclesiology was the eclecticism of the Park Lodges and houses.* Nos. 12-14 *later in date.* No. 16. *Restrained and diginified. Italianate. Symmetrical. Recent dormers.*

Part of the open area of the Upper Park is occupied by a layout of bedding, etc. out of character with Paxton's conception.

Castellated Lodge. *Irregular, with battlements, square tourelles, battlemented chimneys, octagonal staircase tower. Again good detailing though the style results in less refinement than at other of the lodges. The sort of thing Pugin lampooned, and although close in spirit to picturesque Georgian style-mongering, it betrays its Victorian date in its heaviness and solidity. Norman Lodges (East and West.) A chaste Greek-Revival pair. Bi-axially symmetrical, with single-storey and wings. Doric porches in antis. Unusual upper windows in the form of horizontal panels - logical in this context.*

Nos. 2-3, Cavendish Road. *Semi-detached pair. Seen across arm of Upper Lake provides an instance of perimeter housing happily related to landscape.* No.1 Cavendish Road. *(Park Cottage). A simple, irregular house reminiscent of the 'picturesque utility' of the best Victorian parsonage manner and beautifully sited at an important position within the circulation system. Opposite is* Central Lodge. *Pilastered single-storey wing abutting against a block with rusticated ground floor and pilastered upper storey. A composition of great subtlety, and with detailing as good as that of Italian Lodge. Perhaps the most perfect of all the several lodges. Beyond, in Lower Park, a fine view of Cannon Hill.* No.1 Ashville Road. *Italianate. Late 1850s or early 1860s. The central part of Ashville Road, to south, was never intended to be built up, and later planting in Upper Park has destroyed Paxton's uninterrupted views and the effect of continuous landscape between Lower and Upper Parks.*

APPENDIX 'H'

Some of the residents of the new property neighbouring the park, c.1860.

Ashville Road.	Emit Hottie — merchant.
	James Moncrieff Wilson. Manager. Insurance Company.
	Walker Butterworth. General broker.
	Robert W. Dalglish. Merchant.
	Thomas Hogg. Road Surveyor.
	Rev. David T. Barry. B.A.
	William Hind. Merchant. 'Ashville'.
	John H. Hind. Merchant. 'Ashville'.
	Thomas Martin Blythe. Merchant. 'Woodville'.
	Mrs. Higgins.
	John Park. Iron Merchant. 'Elm House'.
	Mrs. Eliza Jane Goodwin.
	William Spalding. Merchant.
	William Anderson. Merchant.
'The Park'.	Edward Whitnall. Printseller.
	Thomas Simonds. Gentleman.
	Rev. John Thomas Pearse. M.A.
Cavendish Road.	Edward Charles Hawker. Merchant.
	Mrs. James Brancker
	John C. Blythe. Merchant. 'Park Villas'.
	Charles Gray Mott. Coal merchant. 'Sunnyside'.
Castle Lodge.	Edward Perrin.
Norman Lodge East.	Charles Staley. Commercial Traveller.
Norman Lodge West.	John Pennington. Cashier.
Park Road South.	Percy Matthew Dove. 'Castleton Lodge'.
	Charles Edward Eaton. 'Abbott's Grange'.
	Robert Fell. 4, Cannon Hill.
	Elias Gaskell. 3, Cannon Hill.
	Richard Gaskell. 2, Cannon Mount.
	Alan Ker. 'Barone Villa'.
	James Macdonald. 'Ennerdale Lodge'.
Park Road West.	Richard Francis Jones. 'Fir Grove'.
	Edward Kemp. Parks' Superintendent.
	William Griffiths Leete. 'Woodleigh'.

BIBLIOGRAPHY

Parks and Cemetries Committee Minutes —
  Book 6 commencing 1891
  Book 8 commencing 1905
  Book 10 commencing 1912
  Book 11 commencing 1918

"History of the Hundred of Wirral"	*William Mortimer*	1847
"Life of Sir William Jackson" ———	*- reprinted from the 'Liverpool Mercury'*	1876
"Memories of Birkenhead"........	*Hilda Gamlin*	1892
"History of Birkenhead"	*P. Sully*	1893
"Birkenhead and its Surroundings".	*H.K. Aspinall*	1903
"Auld Lang Syne"	*Harry B. Neilson*	1939
"The Romance of Wirral"........	*A.G. Caton*	1947
"Birkenhead Yesterday and To-day"	*W.R.S. McIntyre*	1948
"Works of Sir Joseph Paxton 1803-1865"	*George F. Chadwick*	1961
"The Park and the Town"	*George F. Chadwick*	1966
"The Buildings of England. Cheshire"	*Sir Nikolaus Pevsner & Edward Hubbard*	1971

* * * * *

Mawdsley's directory for Wirral. 1861. 1864.
Electoral Roll for Birkenhead. 1864.
"Laws Re Fishing in Park Lakes" — 1889.
Birkenhead Park Byelaws. 1907. B.C.III 343/B.C.III 404.
Memorandum of Birkenhead Park. Victorian Society. "Architectural Review" — April 1967.
Notes by Edward Hubbard prepared for a Victorian Society/ Birkenhead History Society Walk. 28th July 1973. Revised May, 1975.

* * * * *

Liverpool Mercury. (microfilm) — Early part of 1847.
Newpaper Cutting — "Illustrated London News" — April 10th 1847.
Newspaper Cutting — "Birkenhead News" — March 9th, 1968.

* * * * *

Letter from Alan Williams. New Brighton Cycling Club. 24th March 1971.
Letter from Walter Gott. Birkenhead Park Football Club. 7th April 1971.

ACKNOWLEDGEMENTS

The writer would like to record her appreciation for the ready help she has received from Mr. Edward Hubbard, co-author of 'The Buildings of England. Cheshire', and for permission to draw from his notes — (see Appendix G).

She also wishes to thank the Friends of Birkenhead Park for their interest and contributed material; and Mr. John Emmerson of the Birkenhead History Society.

Lastly she would renew her thanks to staff of the Birkenhead Reference Library, Borough Road, also to staff in the Park's Superintendent's Office, for the help they afforded for the writer's original study in 1971.

Some questions to ask yourself when you are in the park.

If Paxton had lived in our time do you think he would have designed Birkenhead Park differently? Supposing you had to design a park! ... Do you think parks are as important today as they were to the nineteenth century town dwellers?

Notice the people who are using the park. Do they belong predominantly to any particular age groups? Are they 'promenading' — perhaps exercising dogs — taking a rest — enjoying a chat with acquaintances? Are there any mothers wheeling prams or pushchairs? Perhaps they have toddlers eager to see and feed the water fowl — or children on the swings? Do you think some people could be using the park as a convenient crossing place to get to work or to school? Maybe they're on their way to Park Station or crossing the other way to get to the shopping precinct? Are there any young people in the park — playing football, or cricket, or fishing?

See if you can locate the Logan Stone in the Lower Park. Nearby is Cannon Hill Terrace. There is a modern building next to it. Do you like this new building or do you prefer the architecture of Cannon Hill? Which building would you prefer to live in? Does the new building 'enhance the view' from the Park?

Visit some of the Lodges. Can you locate the Gothic Lodge or the Castellated Lodge? What about the Norman Lodges or the Italian one? Which ones can you identify? Does any of this architecture appeal to you? Take a look at the two cricket pavilions in the Lower Park. They're very different from each other. Built in different centuries do you consider one to be more functional than the other?

Walk down to the Main Entrance into the park. Do you like it? Do you think it is suitable?

Are there any unusual birds about? Can you identify any of the trees? Do you suppose any of them might have been planted by Mr. Edward Kemp or his gardeners in the mid-nineteenth century? Can you guess which of the Oak trees were planted to mark the Coronations of our Sovereigns? They stand a little apart from the other trees. At one time they had plaques and were protected by railings.

FRIENDS OF BIRKENHEAD PARK

Founded in 1976, this Association is recognised by The Merseyside County Council, Wirral Borough Council and other national societies, as the official conservation group for the protection of Birkenhead Park. All planning applications relating to the park, its periphery buildings and roads are submitted to the committee for its approval.

During recent years, the money allocated under the inner urban grants scheme has helped to restore the park to its present state after a period of neglect. The 'friends' were closely involved in the decisions on how this money was spent. The Wirral Council's Department of Leisure Services and other departments keep in constant touch with the 'friends' and joint meetings are held on park matters.

The Birkenhead Park is our heritage, one which we must pass on to the future citizens in a worthwhile and beautiful state.

If you are interested, join 'The Friends'. Take part in its activities — and help to preserve this beauty spot in the middle of industrial Birkenhead.